It Will Have Been So Beautiful

Amanda Shaw

LILY POETRY REVIEW BOOKS

For Ruth

and Ruthie

While we regret that the past is not like the present and despair of its ever becoming the future, its innumerable inscrutable habits lie in wait for their meaning. I want to gather them, like somebody's grandmother putting up preserves, because they will have been so beautiful.

*

Nothing is ever the same as what they said it was. It's what I've never seen before that I recognize.

–Diane Arbus

Contents

1   And the stars

I. What They Said It Was

5   Ensconced
7   These Mountains (I)
9   Tra voi sapró dividere
12 Love at 24
14 Far From New Hampshire
15 A Peaceable Kingdom

II. This is Not a Bowl

21 Residuum
23 Ceci N'est Pas un Bol
26 Allegory of the Chair
27 Allegory of the Thumb
29 Spring, Room 210
30 For the Bright Choir
33 Langdon Place

III. Design

37 Felis Felix
38 Terremoto
40 You Don't Need a Weatherman
42 The Skiff and the Reef
44 *Make This a Poem*
45 Allegory of the Fish
47 I Hold With Those Who Favor Ice
48 Invasive
49 Swiss National Day

IV. Dance, Dance, Evolution

53   Past Perfect

54   Fifth Moon Out

55   Ruthie's Art

56   These Mountains (II)

58   Dance, Dance, Evolution

61   These Mountains (III)

64   Heart Poetica

V. Far From New Hampshire

66   Love at 48

67   Nothing but Water

69   The Old Man and the Hills

71   Why do you squander/Why do you hoard?

74   Vigil

76   Ashes, Ashes

78   Where We Are

And the stars

In and out of the pull of Saturn, towards
a ribbon-thin gap in its majestic rings

Cassini flies through full-fathomed dark
in a choreographed series of turns

tracing ellipses among moons and ice.

Headlines today, beside the newest record heat,
of a possible second genesis

       out of little Enceladus:
phosphorous dust in lunar seas.

Another arc, oh dome of the sky,
may it be far enough

from each day's loss. From the lupine and the fireweed,
the fleet trail of the flight

of every winged bird of every kind.

I.
What They Said It Was

Why should
These mountains being high be, also, bright,
Fetched up with snow that never falls to earth?

Wallace Stevens, "The Dove in the Belly"

Ensconced

At the mall or by mail, from Pottery Barn
or the like, you can buy a way to soften glare
and call it design. Lest tallow spill or candles flare

or a torch burn entire towns, settlers left a coast
of saltboxes hugging the shore
and went West—built a road to everywhere

to arrive at the lightbulb. Now, progress
is the end of a time zone echoing
down the wide avenues, a man hailing the bus

that's left him behind. It's mornings
that arrive two hours late, long past
the bright New England dawn.

When I didn't know what she meant
when she asked me what I meant by "home,"
my mother decided to send me sun

in a box. Our last New Hampshire winter,
my brother and I marched and marched
around the frigid farmhouse, singing along

with Tigger and Piglet and Pooh
bouncy, trouncy, ouncey, pouncy,
                    fun fun fun fun fun

until the day my father broke the record.
Home, now, is a cell phone's
You cannot undo this action. It's kitchen islands

and central air, rooms so tall
I can't open cupboards or reach
the recessed lights. Home, now, our walls

are thin. Neighbors all down the long halls
can hear I'm playing this song
again and again. That love calls me

and I've no place to hide.
Mother, I mean this guitar flaring out
its plangent chords, the five o'clock shadow

at the closed window. I heard it, just once,
not long after we left, on a cheap radio—
the strain of my father's old harmonies,

and my hands loosened. I mean:
I want nothing more than to love that way,
without shade—a naked beach in a storm,

a ledge of resonant sea—
not splintered knees or crooked floors
or a girl affixed to her father's legs

as he tried to kick her away—
not that, her cheek against the cold
linoleum, the careless fluorescence

of his gaze. The soft glow, the carpeted fall.
This song. This song. I want back that girl
with nothing more than to love.

These Mountains (I)

In the Cathedral of Lausanne, what Europe couldn't give me
is caught in the picture I hoped you'd take but didn't—

young woman pale at the altar, gaze cast down
like the dove's, translucent rose watering the stone behind.

Below were lakes too large to lose their blue, the clipped fists
of plane trees in winter, and the Musée de L'Art Brut

where you showed me Aloïse's love affairs in crushed petals
and toothpaste, the *paysages alpestres* of the Appenzeller orphan

(Master of the UHT Carton), and the terrified horse, assembled
from sticks and brambles. Europe was cold. I'd brought the wrong

coat; in your mother's I grinned, tongue thick in my Anglophone
mouth, all tufts and peakless rounds each time you tried a portrait.

On the way to Montana, a state I thought green and cradling,
the craggy valleys and slopes we climbed and climbed

scathed the unseen from my mind. You took
me from your grandparents' house to the edge to hear

the Swiss village quaking softly below, its glacial pace
unruffled by the heights. *L'art brut*, I later learned,

Americans call by a gentler name, *Outsider*. We're wrong.
The twisted twigs that cried out horse, the masks of red rag

and yarn, the luminous cramped manuscripts: a flame of tongues
sharp as mountains in the brute January night. Last week,

some old urge waked in you, and you insisted: Amanda in thought
in rain, in Michigan, a state without hills for miles and miles.

The camera is a manageable fate. That first ghost-image
of your rag-and-yarn girl, your Aloïse muffled in a rush of down—

look for it now, you'll find I erased it long ago. What remains:
your language without euphemism, your funicular, perched,

spired country. The place you'd keep me if I fell.

Tra voi sapró dividere…

Campo de' Fiori, Rome

The telephone rings, notes flat,
from another country. Voices
in the slate and stuccoed hall.

The water tank maintains
its stasis: heat spent, heat gained.
I know its periodic sleep,

know it waits for me
to wash ink-stains from sheets
or cleanse hair of oil, skin of cells

the body's left behind. I eat
food without season, oatmeal
and foil-sealed bars; keep

irradiated milk, measured
by the milliliter. The feet
forget the feel of shoes.

I've learned the street's
routine: mornings, a door recedes
into a warehouse ceiling, its metal

cantankerous and slow. Wiry men
load wheeled wooden carts
with trinkets for the market;

they sing and bark and snap
but mostly laugh.
Hoisting buckets of cut flowers

onto his wagon, a neighbor sings
libiamo amor fra i calici
che la bellezza infior—

as the motor of his aging scooter
crackles and spits.
Santa Brigida's quartered hours

chime and toll: *prime, terce*, none:
not soon enough…not long enough
before they're summoning the clatter

back. Brigades of small trucks
gather discarded wares
in the pink of the afternoon square,

someone's heels up stone stairs,
the oak door's ancient latch
reversing once, twice, a final thud

as the murmur from the piazza
rises to din. Obsequious greeters
cajole tourists, buskers hustle,

childhood friends chatter
in their mother tongue.
In the narrow alley in the waning night,

the occasional shatter
—bottles on the cobblestone—
and then it all begins again.

This is what it means
to be alone, to lie in a cloister
unsleeping, to listen to what

I wouldn't hear if speaking
and think of all I've left unsaid, to hope
that one of these quarter-hours

I might unseal myself
and venture out into the hall
to tell the neighbor his arias are sweet

or try that phone once more—
        This is what it means

to think better of it, to know
an answered call won't make the tongue
less strange to any ears. To retreat

to the whitewashed walls
whose blemishes I know so well
and listen for the purring of the heater.

Love at 24

And that's it: the ear attuned
to silences, a locked canal
  leading to the throat. Sore,

I try to speak, it just gets
  worse. But also, sometimes, soaring—
a vision of when the love was new,

  dropped in my path. Late
to work, unable to walk
  past a broken bird; looking

for a shoebox, anything
  to keep alive what's going
to dwindle to oblivion. And I

  was happy. It's the original
pathetic fallacy. Wings break;
  birds die; a decade later

I'm waking up to *I'd do you
  in a houseboat. Or have you do me*—
change of subject. He wishes

  he could be funny
in the deep way, not so foolish,
  and I think he is; he makes

me laugh. Saddest thing in the world,
  to fail to laugh
when someone you love thinks a joke

  is really funny. Sad, but
funny, like falling out of the boat
  that was going to take us

back. Was going to call, forgot.
 Didn't want to? Memory recalls
the phone quiet, recalls

 the inflamed throat. Who knows
what I'd have said? Instead,
 I kept myself from telling him

the saddest funny thing I read today,
 a doctor repeating a man's last words:
not *I love you* or a name on his lips

but a rasp, "Oh fuck, oh fuck."
Love: today I looked for houseboats,
 which can float or move slowly

downriver via canals. They can go far
 but not very fast; most canals
don't get that deep. You'll get much further

 flying, which we'd have to do
if we want to see each other
 and there's nowhere left

to land—it's one deep thing
 we never have to say. How we both love
water, though; running, sluicing,

 shining; even brine. Once we needed it
so badly, sitting in the car
 after years apart, we had to stop

and I drank
 that big gulp in one long swallow
and still wanted more.

Far from New Hampshire

As children we must have often walked
along the low stone walls
on the way to Mrs. Foote's orchard, and yes,

I see my brother
seared by light in a field of weeds
contemplating a perfect buttercup

and in my hand a milkweed pod,
seed-floss tinged with green and clinging—

my brother who though a gentle boy
terrorized the kitten we got as consolation
after the divorce

picking her up again and again
until she hid for days
and I was furious.

He kept saying he was trying not to
but couldn't help it
and I knew it,

he had a little too much love in him
and the count of who he had to give it to
was down; but see

I'd suffered the same
diminution
and just because he was smaller

I had to learn to let the kitten go
so he could learn to move on.

A Peaceable Kingdom

No, not that one, let's move
      on; this country will give us no
            peace. Let's go where May tadpoles

turn to June crickets keening,
      the starlight glimmering, July heat
            made sound. I mean the country

where we used to live
      when snow drifts outweighed a child,
            made monolithic hedges, narrowed

the dirt path home. I'm too small
      to see above them, or beyond.
            Soon the men who tap trees

will collect their tin buckets, speaking
      gruffly and seldom. March will snow on
            into April, sometimes May, receding at last

to late-awakening loam. August,
      Queen Anne's lace. Like light
            pressed to the back of the closed lid

when you nap on a slope
      among hollowing stalks of fall. Fall,
            the last country. The country on a hill.

Sometimes I pretend it's all been down
      from there. I mean the country, not
            my life. A country of four seasons,

fall and spring brief but discrete:
        that was true, before winters too warm
                for what used to be May. Before

summer in November.
        I haven't given the months
            in order, but I've tried to make it

beautiful. I'm trying, and it was. It's just
        the dark green staircase creaked
                a captive unicorn lurking

on the landing, shushing *Go back*
        to bed. The bed in my room, my room
                next to the old birthing room

where my father's easel perched, waiting
        for his revision. The birthing room
                that smelled of linseed, siren-sweet

turpentine—rich smells that made me
        tiptoe past, day-times, while he worked
                on a copy of a Quaker masterpiece,

an American triumph, a copy
        of a scene Hicks painted again and again:
                sixty-two times, by historians' count.

On my father's moonlit canvas,
        small swirls of brown hinted bull;
                yellow ochre, leopard; stencils

foretold the startled lion
        and insomniac lamb.
                Hicks so hoped

for a new era—his children
would play with snakes,
the lion deny the carnal,

lie quiet beside the sleeping lamb.
On my father's canvas
only the background scene

would wind up complete, a white man
offering the Lenape a small-
pox infected red blanket

with a smile. I want to believe
this man doesn't know
what he comes bearing,

what they accept: I believe he's truly
thinking it's peace. What bright eyes
on Hicks's great ox, looking at me

now. No, I couldn't have known
it was a copy of a copy. The red velvet
a pestilence. The cloth, it looks so soft.

II.

This is Not a Bowl

Residuum

"Detritus? I've never heard that word,"
my new neighbor says, as I'm apologizing for what
I mistakenly rinsed off of my deck onto his below,
　　　　　the stems and leaves and plastic labels they stick in the dirt
at a plant nursery, the ones that tell you whether you possess
the suitable conditions for keeping the poor root-
bound flowers alive wherever you're taking them, which in
my case I do, enough light and space for roots to spread and choice
of deck or windowsill or yard depending on weather or time of year
　　　　　and I answer "You know, 'DEH-

bris,'" the way the English guy in a thousand-part documentary
about excavations at Troy (that whole *Today I have gazed upon the face
　of Agamemnon*) says
　　　　　"de-bREE," as though my neighbor, Steve,
who doesn't know me or the word detritus—and he's a lawyer—
would know why that foppery is funny, that I'd never
say the word that way myself except as a joke (the kind I tell
that never land), although when I was ten I'd say "malice of
　　　　　forethought" or "beating a dead horse" and my friends were like

What the fuck Amanda, but see now I'm forty-five and live next to
lawyers and have the space and light to grow flowers in nourishing but
messy soil, that
　　　　　detritus that washes down onto
his deck in spite of my care; no, he's got to know I'm not *that*
weird, moreover I've heard it said I'm a "cute nerd," that's how far
I've come, but Steven's gay anyway and surely my level of cute-despite-
awkward-ness isn't in play, I'm just saying I'm not that person, I'd never
deliberately fling soil—lets face it, *dirt,* it's trash, it's

　　　　　detritus, it's just the right word
for the situation—onto his property, incidentally that mofo Schliemann
was not only wrong about Agamemnon, he dug all that dirt up without

forethought, destroyed the layers of time above the find he bragged
about with such grandiosity, but I know enough now not to share this further
evidence of nerdity so I am furiously digging into my mind like I always do for

        words, more words
to supplement the more words that didn't work the first time
        but then Steven says "I like it. I'll have to use it"
and I kneel down to pet his little dog Stacy who is truly adorable even when
she barks at me from the debris I've washed onto his deck below,
        I mean who can blame her?

Ceci N'est Pas un Bol

A woman in Italy is selling the bowl
   on my mother's table. An auction house
in Dallas has a set of three, on sale
   for thousands less. 19th Century Bowls

in Classic Clover Pattern—they live
   in a warehouse (or on a screen):
the clover is hard to see. Our clover lives
   on my mother's marble table (not mine,

it's glass). These Classic Bowls,
   they must be full
of untold memories, not mine.
   Our bowl has always been empty,

polished but tarnished
   where the slender vines entwine;
rim in full silver flower,
   rich concavities a tulip's wide bloom.

Centuries back, in Holland,
   a certain kind of unplanted bulb
was worth an entire economy
   if you knew how to translate time

into currency, currency into time.
   With time, a bowl cast in silver
appreciates—more if it's Tiffany, less
   if dirtied or dinged

or marked with a family's curlicued *M*,
   like mine. *With all that went on,*
my mother asks, *who kept it safe?*
   You can't find the answer

online. Grocers sell heirloom
   tomatoes; florists, heirloom
bulbs (though tulips we mostly buy
   cut)

but never again the *Semper Augustus*,
   a flower that made a country mad. "Tulip-
omania," they called it, before
   the bubble burst: like the craze, the bulbs

were "broken" by disease. Tiffany Tulips
   in favrile glass, petals rimmed in lead, adorn
museum windows; you can buy
   reproductions in shops. The *Semper*

Augustus, however, is gone:
   speculators named it "always,"
then killed the species off.
   I've never been to Dallas; Italy

was years ago. Clover grows here,
   among wild grasses, but not
our Clover, it's silver. "Serving Bowl,"
   the Italian calls hers, praising

its preserved curves, its patina;
   to me, refractions just look like glare.
Whoever wanted it
   to be a "Bowl"? I want only

the way it used to hold the porous light
   of winter afternoons. Over a century ago,
Tiffany & Co.
   cast millions of vines in relief,

thousands of clovers to skirt the rims
  of hundreds of sterling silver bowls;
ca. 1898, my great-
  grandmother received one

for her wedding—no one knows
  what was served, or on what table,
let alone how it survived. Worth
  thousands to someone; to another,
thousands less. *All that*: it will be mine.

Allegory of the Thumb

for Cleo

Vibrating like a purr cut short,
a text—again, the pharmacy, Reply

Y if you do, N if you don't need more
of the steroid and its tiny syringe

to titrate the viscous stuff
made to shrink whatever blot

was distorting the messages to her spine
in a terrible game of telephone. Gone

the pure quiet her murmur created
around itself. In the end I held the legs

that couldn't kick, the thumb
that rubbed her ears for all her years

pressed to her trachea
until she choked the liquid down.

I know I answered STOP. She's dander
in the dustpan, fur in the dryer lint, she's

what her sister smells in the leftover toys.
What medicine she managed to refuse

remained in the fur on her cheek
her paw no longer knew how to clean

as I pet her in our sleep.

Allegory of the Chair

My aunt was drunk at the table when she said
(pitched a bit too far towards
the edge of the chair and leaning
even closer to my boyfriend) *I have read*
a great deal of Plato, some of it
in the original Greek

                   —and one late night
parked in my boyfriend's driveway
when I told him his hair smelled like Play-Doh,
yeasty, nourishing against my mouth
in his dark truck, he murmured
Some of it in the original
and we laughed, not so much at her
as at the memory of a silent film
our Western Civ teacher had shown us,
in which a small fat man sits chained to a chair
watching ciphers and odd shapes dance
on a sweating cave wall
until he escapes into the wide blue world—

neither of us could remember how,
but he returns an apostle, tries
to persuade his fellow cavemen
the world they think is real
is just a flimsy negative, a mirage, a form
like you have to fill out at the dentist's
or the DMV (or that whole sheaf of papers
they give you at a hospital); he's raving
at them, waving his arms
at the shadows on the wall, panting
and sweating from the effort
but his brothers don't want to hear;
they turn on him, beat him with his chair
until FINI, THE END—

We were supposed to be moved
because look how man chooses illusion, turns
violently from knowledge—
but what was the filmmaker thinking,
or our teacher? We were fifteen. And it *was*
funny, the way she'd said *in the original*,
but even then I knew
what she wanted my boyfriend to know—
that she cared about thought, the life
of the mind;

I don't know what she felt like drunk
but sometimes when I am I think
my intelligence is surging,
my language floating up
in plumes of heat above the clouds
and the whispering clear nowhere,
I think I see fields grow architectural,
cities rise, clean morning precede
the blown-open night
and I just have to explain
to anyone who's there
how form and pure idea cohere

but then you sober up, it's just a chair,
my aunt's still dead; she died not long after
that scene at the dining room table,
I saw her in the hospital, her skin
was green, stretched over her hardened liver
(hardened not unlike old Play-Doh
after a child has grown bored)—she
expired, she passed, she's no longer
with us, she went up in flame
like a strip of celluloid, as though
the projectionist had turned away
instead of loading the next reel.

Spring, Room 210

I have moved the desk. The test
I've been given   stretches
 over eleven pages   of choices;

on some I'm provided a box
where I'm to pencil in   a sketch.

The taut vowels of men salting the steps
slip through gaps

into my room.   Out the locked window it's
April in Vermont
and I am
                    away.

With the desk here, from a certain angle,
I can focus
on last October's leaves

graven on the skin of the ice
still skimming the Connecticut.

Earth burgeoning outside
these two-hundred-year-old panes
revoke your newest confessions

your crocuses
                    I never meant to

For the Bright Choir

When Gandalf said to the ancient earth-beast
    You   Shall   Not   Pass
it worked, they fell through fire,

beast and wizard, the Fellowship escaping
into the snow. And the music swelled
and characters mourned

and we were confused that Peter Jackson
or Tolkien would kill the mentor off
so soon. And so a year later

when the wizard re-appeared,
when the screen blaring with white
lit up a boy's face as he cried out
       GAN-dalf!

we all felt the joy in the drawn-out rise
and fall of his little syllables,
his great surprise magnified

by the year of stricken silence—
you might have paid him for it,
the boy beating back sorrow

in that white glow.
Later, I remembered Ian McKellen
as though he were the other all-

seeing wizard, falling
fathoms off a stone tower
after the deepest kind of betrayal—

the kind we should have seen coming—
the unkindest wand-blow of all,
so hard it made me stumble off the plane

and into my husband's arms
only to find myself before I even said hello
blurting out *Snape killed Dumbledore.*

By then everyone knew the wizard died
but not by whose hand. My husband,
confused and a little frustrated, held

me anyway, because I'd finished the book
in my narrow seat towards the back
(economy row, no status) while

my no-status neighbor kept talking
though Harry was sitting at the funeral
thinking The Last of my Great Protectors

is Gone. *Who do you think will leave you,*
Greg asked me once; *Who*
is going to betray you? and I didn't know;

some staff had come down hard
before I went plunging into a core of earth
and burned and girlhood never re-appeared

but I could have used his light-flooded face,
that boy surprised into song, beside me
in that cramped seat on that cramped plane

that always left at night and arrived at dawn,
compressing the dark so arrival felt
like I'd never had the chance to disappear—

his small body beside me in a spring-sick seat,
cheaper than the theater's lumpy vinyl slab
from which he'd seemed to leap

through the dark, leaving
the sticky floor and stale butter
for those of us grown heavy

in our middle rows. That bright face
to keep my neighbor to himself
(You shall not pass

between the mourner and her grief),
keep the secret to myself, or at least
allow Greg's arms to hold it safe.

Langdon Place

My mother's neighbor wishes I wouldn't go
    so soon, see, here's the labyrinth

she walked as her grandson drew it,
    the perfect circles he showed her

when she finished the path she thought
    they'd shared. And I see how well

he's rendered where she'd have had to stop
    if she'd chosen her first turn wrong.

I want to talk about Chartres, the ancient stone
    worn slick so you know where to step

but her phone rings in time. *If you love art,*
    she calls, come back. To say *I do*

might mean *I will*, which verges on cruel. Still,
    I'd like to tell her grandson she's right;

he's talented—that down a hall of the angry phonemes
    Fox calls news, her quiet door beckons, floors

unpolished but genuine pine: she lives,
    my mother lives, at one of the good ones.

III.
Design

I kept no record of my failures, for I had many. The main thing was to assure some success by trying many things and holding on to the plants, which had learned that life is worth holding on to even at its bitterest.

—F. Reichel, gardener and prisoner at Alcatraz

Felis Felix

At night kitty climbs, descends, returns
to our bed. Morning's just a change
of light and human stumbles—
toast and tea, assembly of keys,
coats, purse, IDs. Litter sifted, water new,
same dry crumbles in her dish, she'll chew
a bit and then emerge, surveilling
our departure. Days I'm home I watch
the busy ears despite apparent sleep,
registering idling engines, a swallow's
impertinent twaddle. Windowsill and deck
present a neighbor's ledge, the pesky squirrel
who always evades her just in time.
No matter: soon her mewling will subside
to purrs, curl of soft limbs in a tight circle,
queen of the warmest spot
on bed, chair, or floor. Her humans sleep
a human sleep, a nightly scrubbing
of memory; we awaken to stiffness
and chores, flowers uprooted
by the goddamn squirrel;
begin our fumbling way once more.
Though not gifted with a range of sound
she lets us know with her clean tongue
You'll never own your lives as I do mine,
however well you open doors.

Terremoto

Italy, August 2016

Rieti rests in the hum of dusk, spires backlit
in muted rose. Far below the earth's crust shifts

and centuries are gone.
Look at this picture of the empty air

where roofs once were,
the Mayor says to the world,

Amatrice non c'é piu:
Amatrice is no more

*

Half a truss saws
against a placid sky,
the Apennines an icy witness.

The photographer can't help
himself: blood on her wimple,

Sister Marjana of the Order
of the Handmaids of the Lord

slumps in the road, looking down
at her cell phone. Broken

icon, broken asphalt. By these
we shall know Thee

*

God,

what a landscape. A jagged
half of a home

a cracked dome
and an azure sky

crumbled on chapel flagstone

*

The blue sky
felt lonely, its wrath

not up to the task:
look how well the earth

can smite
—the sun outmatched

by the mother's hot core

*

Lord, behold your newest map,
the faultlines you've made.
Look upon the earth's

cracked crown,
Your devotee searching

for news of Your mercy
on a broken phone

You Don't Need a Weatherman

to tell you that it's hotter than the Summer
of Love. After they cut back the old forest,
the brook in Stowe that used to turn
my mother's skin scarlet from shock
began to sun itself like any winter being
released at last from shade, now it's a naiad

of a former earth. "The War was so big
we didn't know what to do," says a weathered
Mark Rudd: turns out the kids did need
a forecast; they thought they'd find a wind
to blow the racist fuckers off the map
but we were always heading South

and after a century of New York's trash
a landfill in the Meadowlands has grown so hot
it's frying birds. Come *on*, mothers and fathers;
Telemachus, if you believed your dad who said
(before he sailed off into the West) All experience
is an arch, you have to strive to seek to find

you'll be angry when you come to understand
the earth is round—you meet old triumphs
in the ass. It's not a pretty sight, that ass, fallen
like Brigitte Bardot's after decades
of more gravity than we should have to face
and here we are each summer breaking

records. Is Bardot still alive? Mark Rudd's
a math teacher in the desert. My husband says
aren't you glad no child of yours
will ask if you were pretty once, as I asked my mom
when I was nine—no child of mine
will have to guess which way that wind is blowing
by its foul smell. No one to throw my ashes
in the brook my mother loved, becoming a river of fire.

The Skiff and the Reef

The television is tuned to a show
about Britons fishing in a kind of skiff

made of interwoven willow-rods
and I'm not really listening until I hear

it's called a *coracle*, a pretty word
that after I turn the TV off

plays on in my head, sea-changed
to *Coral kill*, the flap in my mind

that opens to this odd sentence
like the flap in the pop-up book

I gave Ruthie who lives by the sea,
a flap which you can lift to see

the pink stinging branches snaking up—
Watch out, poor fish!

At first I wondered what I'd done
but Ruthie told me not to worry,

Daniel Tiger told her Grown-Ups
Come Back, *Him mommadadda save him,*

it's ok. First time I watched *Daniel Tiger*
the chirpy four notes of his chirpy song

stuck in my head for the rest of the day
and I was almost angry at the lie. See,

Ruthie doesn't know about this yet
but kids in her mother's first grade class

are going home to find it dark,
Mommadadda disappeared to Mexico

and never coming back.
                    I've no reason to doubt

Poor Fish's parents taught him well,
made sure he washed his sticky gills

then tucked him into weeds each night,
might swim up in the nick of time

to save him from the poisoned reef—
but Ruthie, that flap could open

to anything, right to the bottom
of the rising sea. What about

the Britons? what about the shark.

Make this a poem

October first, the raw air tempting the cats
to a truce, burying
battle lines in the duvet's down. It's Sunday:
no calls to doctors

I have to convince to help, no promises
to Medi-swear-to-god
she's worth the money. Down the road
someone's mowing,

adult children gather next door; late-season bees
drowsing and curious
mean a grandchild is going to cry. Tractors,
manure: weekends

just a different set of chores—
Dust banisters, Empty litter, Mop floor.
My hands are drying out. These little brats,
they're "geriatric"—

fourteen years ago someone found them
in a wall, together, mewling
and kittenhood was shared in tiny baskets.
Now their fights

are so pitched I think I'm hearing tomcats
squaring off in the night
which is already too cold for September.
Tomorrow I'll promise myself

in unwritten lists *Buy lotion, Call Care Coordinator,*
Find gloves/scarves/hats
while Ginger, whose husband couldn't die at home,
feeds the last hummingbirds.

Allegory of the Fish

Some years ago now someone found CelexaBenaZoAbilify
norfluoxine venlafaxine diphenhydramine paroxetine
in Great Lakes fish brains fish livers fish muscles even gonads

and reading about this I remembered Roger and Me
was set in Flint not far from Lake Huron, the very same city
where decades later it all came out some nameless guys

had led its residents to tainted water
then claimed they weren't the ones who made the people drink.
"Besides, we all die anyway," I believe is how it went down

at the hearing, which only just happened a month or so
ago; though the spokesman had a point: we're all drinking
something that'll kill us

                  microplastics arseniphosphate chlor-

insectipesticide, which reminds me I think it's weird
the French call weeds *mauvaises herbes*, "bad grasses":
it seems *les botanistes* neglected to ask the honeybees

and pretty soon it'll be too late. At first I didn't understand
how antidepressants would make the poor Great-Lake-shrimp
suicidal: turns out Prozac led them toward the light

where it just so happens their predators hang out. But back
down in the weeds I'm thinking any bee would tell the French
Don't blame the damn plants:

everything wants to find a way to come back
though the factory or the jobs Roger took from Flint
never did. Fun fact, the government sent truckloads of water

Nestle's draining the Great Lakes to sell
but it was nowhere near enough to help them drink
all those years away, now the babies weaned on trihalomethanes

are schoolgirls and boys struggling to make it
through third grade—though even if they could they'd find
the teachers themselves are barely hanging on. Maybe

it's time for a sequel to Roger and Me
which was a pretty good movie Michael Moore
but you didn't need to show me the rabbit

alive   flayed

        jerking

I Hold With Those Who Favor Ice

Azure beneath titanium white,
floes slower than forever,

I mimic what I am becoming,
what I was.

    You open your guidebooks. You hike.

Through holes in thinning clouds
sun calves me, mercurial,
cleaving, widening crevasses.

    You pick at me, make me a mirror,
      make me World Heritage,
      make me Before/After
      in shocking montage.

Stop talking
about lonely planets
wet-bulb-heat real-feel
AQI. What do you know

of after? I negate myself, waves
returning to waves,
lap at your cities   mock your maps.

Invasive

Again I forgot my gloves
and the nosy neighbor always calls
when I'm pulling life from the ground.
He'd hate the dirt
on my rough hands: give him a planet

he'd have employees wipe pollen
from new leaves
& last year's mulch, make them sift
basalt from sand, bring him the white
dollars left in the sieve

—flakes of abalone, empty mussels
littering the littoral.
Friends, the flotsam on our shores
is plastic,
fuck your ornamental grasses,

leave the stalk
of the gone-to-seed lily. The world created
to comprehend itself
is weedy

I learned
too late, the goldenrod gone, moths
caught in the zapper and monarchs
hungry. Let
a thousand outside insects call
and make us nothing.

Swiss National Day

Lawn sprinkler fanning water out and then

    in long arcs up, catching an angle

        of light in its sway, pausing over roses.

Blackbird extracts a lethargic grub

    through thick bark, a quick lizard flits

        across sun-bleached awning into hedge.

Last year I thought I'd run out of words for green.

    Now in these mined gold valleys

        the flowers supplicate, blossoms

            bowing low above the patchy grass. Dry

heat sleeps by the cool river, soon to roar

    and make us wilt. In the dew

        the neighbor's sprinkler persists,

            a shudder like a catch in the chest

after sobs. She has gone away for the holiday.

    No fireworks in mountain towns. Not this year.

IV.
Dance, Dance, Evolution

Past Perfect

An oleaginous rainbow
floats in the heat
on puddles in the Safeway lot.

Anchor no more, Don Lemon's
muddled his cocktail a bit too long.
If I'm honest, Don, implies you're not.

I've curated this body for mirrors.
My feet are hot, I want something sweet,
the flies are buzzing for rot.

Fifth Moon Out

…and for a time feared speaking lest she moo—Metamorphoses, Ovid

1

Humans can't keep their stories straight.
I'm a cow, I'm a priestess, I'm a moon,
my body's bovine or it's out of this world;
I'm gad-flied and hoofing it
or tracing my name in the dust
while my father's crying *Woe!*
I-O, I-O, off to be milked I go—

2

God, Jupiter's messy, seeding
clouds, raining offspring
over the earth, lording it
over his own Mother
who absorbs his white hot bolts
and toxic spill,
who shoved him in a cavity
to hide him from his father's maw.

3

Watched by a thousand monstrous eyes
or stuck in the gravity of a gaseous giant—
they never let the woman choose
but Ovid, really, "Moo?" Give me
the one where I'm spitting fire
Count my volcanoes Hear me low.

Ruthie's Art

Glitter glue in its gold viscosity
under greedy fingers, oh joy
of the mess, indulgence
of hands—your *Mother*

of the Twelve Fingers
can hold up the sky. *See me!*
you'll cry, dancing a jig
on the beach. *Go too far away!*

and my real arms might reach
to the sea. Sleepovers you wake me at dawn
to shape red paper avatars
of the hearts

unfolding for you. Girl,
that sky is always cornflower blue,
your shark fins come in twos,
whole planets hula or twirl

to whichever off-beat you choose.
Under your dandelion stars
we clap our many-fingered hands

from the good seats:
all the seats
in your new world have views.

These Mountains (II)

Puy de Sancy, France

It is too hot, the innkeeper had warned us,
his English precise, except
for the word for *les moucherons,* the pests
that haunt the salt-rich springs
and pilgrims seeking restoration
of their weakened lungs. Unprepared,
tourists, we walked up a ski trail
to get to the top of the idle dome,
the dust and sharp grade
making me listless, making
the blisters more irksome,
making gravity personal, vindictive.
I could have run up such a slope
in better times—*little mountain
goat,* Greg said, on our first
visits to the Alps.

The grass at the top seemed new enough
—seemed altogether placid. I looked
and looked. Just grass. The French
picnicked and scowled,
children whined. What was I
supposed to feel? Clermont's
famed cathedral made of tuff
had just looked black,
as though grime had broken down
white marble or stone. Up there
amid the midges and wild carrot
Greg told me about the layers of time
I couldn't see, the remnants
of fervent lava streams
beneath the green furrows

and uneven strips of rock. Midges?
Black flies? Gnats? Whatever
the tongue called them, they sought
our hollows, entered nose and mouth.

Thirteen million years ago
the porous earth broke
and heaved trails of molten rock,
leaving the ridges where we sat
watching the flow of pilgrims in shorts
batting at the buzzing clouds.
That evening in Riom, the small flies gone,
we sat on the hotel balcony
looking out in the milder air
over velvet peaks, pyroclastic spires,
and the hot earth's furious fault-lines
—line of tired climbers, line of fire
cooled to leisure: this human
reach, these earthly expirations.

Dance, Dance, Evolution

The so-called waggle dance
confused me at first,
why above her honeycomb a bee
will move for up to one hundred circuits,
wagging her pointy rump
in a perfect figure 8: I thought
the dancer was pointing
to the honey already in the comb;

didn't understand
why the other bees would care.
My husband, amused, explained
how scouts make their bodies into arrows
to guide the hive to pastures new:
it's true: scientists
have mapped the dance on axes,
calculated trajectories

for the vector of her busy jig.
Though the first of many to observe
believed the bees were celebrating
"certain pleasures and jollity," before too long
another showed up and proved it a fact
of survival. I even came across a young linguist
praising us at the bees' expense
"Bees can't speak of honey on the moon,

only the honey they've already seen"
in a tone of triumph
I found absurd. If bees are born
with the skills they'll need to help
the hive, why talk of seeking out
new worlds? Consider
the worker, shaped so well, in perfect thirds—
head, plump thorax and tapering bum,

the pollen baskets on her furry legs
like eco-friendly shopping bags.
To make Greg laugh I tried the dance
and there was much more waggle
than I'd have preferred. Though bees
preserve their figures
efficiently—no single lady dances

without a meadow white with lilies,
a sea of alyssum just over that next hill—
humans, we can't help ourselves,
we'll eat whatever honey
we can get, then run in circles at the gym.
I have to, anyway; last time I danced instinctively
the boys all laughed

and I sat back down. So it's a comfort
to hear there's a dance out there
to save a race from doom,
but wouldn't you know? even the waggle
is up for debate: some swear
it's olfactory factors, not mystic rites
that will rescue the species
from the Varroa mite. The scientists

in this more practical camp warn
a single bee might go on more than 50 runs,
returning so often to a favorite patch
her sisters will learn to ignore
even her most graceful figure 8. And in case
you're the type to hold out hope,
these men are happy to go on
explaining why the dance itself, ergo, is doomed:

"Following social cues takes more energy
than foraging on your own,"

moreover, "transmitted information
quickly becomes obsolete."
Still, given a choice, I'd hold with the guy
who guessed they danced for joy.
Let them return to flowers they've seen:
no bee is going to the moon.

These Mountains (III)

Pays d'Enhaut, Switzerland

Jagged-hemmed
country in bright summer,
    a sheepdog's quick bark
sharpens the quiet

as we float at the seam
    of mountain and sky.
A carillon rises to our far-off ears,
    the cows meandering

across the emerald alpages. From here
    you can't see the drought
which means the beasts will have to descend
    a month early this year—

just the twisting silver of a river
    spilling into shallow lake
that shimmers
    like a hammered coin.

In the next compartment M. Hubert
    murmurs in his broad Vaudois
"How tranquil."
    Mais de Dieu c'est paisible.

He seemed bewildered as we rose
    but with each synonym
his confidence grows. What a wonder,
    what a marvel! and indeed

to all of us
    an impossibility:
        a congress of fire and tissue,
a torch-borne expanse of pied fabric

propelling the human-heavy basket higher
    or easing it lower
as the balloonist wishes.
    He has been doing this so long

he knows the wind
    as the villagers know cows,
the rasp of broad tongues, the muddling
    cuspids, as the cows know the sweet cream

their stomachs can coax from grass:
    no more than each of us needs, it seems,
up here. No more than I need
        —and the thought

hangs there
    longer than expected, long enough
for thought to almost disappear
    but by the fourth—fifth?—time

Monsieur Hubert has sounded his theme
    I'm thanking his wife for reminding him
"It's only tranquil if you stop talking."
    Si tu te tais.

Our hour ends in slow descent.
    The balloon's shadow widens
as we fall, its round top halving
    to form a crenelated heart

against the pines, broadening
    and thinning, until the shade
which held us for this pause
    becomes the balloon again

and with a lurch we regain the ground,
    the sunburned field festooned
with dung, flies tormenting
    the mild-tempered cows.

heart poetica

It is as easy as lying...Look, these are the stops—Hamlet

Flower of vitriol
flower of frost-bite

you'd-play-upon-this-organ heart

rabbit heart   pigeon heart
cotton heart, twine

heart-grub   heart-mite
lipstick, swine,

you tendril, you vine-
heart
you blood blight   love bite

but-you-can't-make-it-sing

iamb-heart   murmur-heart
heart   -beat   -line

—can't-live-with-you,
will-you-or-won't-you

daisy heart seed-heart
rag heart   mine

V.
Far from New Hampshire

...as if there were no such cold thing.

George Herbert, "The Flower"

Love at 48

That boy and I will never clean glass
in the master bath, fully clothed, the dirt
of potted plants floating
at my callused feet. We'll never commiserate

at soap-scum's accumulation
on the *outside* of the doors. Lime for scurvy,
lime in milk, he galvanized
the follicles of my abdomen, we ate

Galapagos turtles, soup spooned
from the shells
of their boiled bodies. We ignored
extinction.

This weekend, the toilet is leaking, source
unknown. That boy
has never returned from the hardware store
with a liquid whose enzymes delight me.

Nothing but Water

Therefore, Ahab stayed below.

The little man who taught us physics
would speak of "liquid water,"
as if we knew it could be otherwise,
or "water ice" might differ
from what we thought was ice itself.
We giggled, as we'd laughed
at the hair that poked its black ends
from his collar or out his nostrils,
as we'd smirked when he shortened
"Newton" to New'n,
the nasal and soft consonant
smoothed so weight was time—
two Newtons, two noons—
a doubled hour in Mis'r Como's lab
spent measuring the properties
of what we thought we knew.

When Peleg asked Ishmael *What do you see?*
the sailor answered in truth: *Nothing
but water.* A nautical maven, still
Melville mistook *under weigh*
for *underway*, switched momentum
and weight, or made them the same,
the captain-heavy ship
weathered by salt and grit
but surpassing her elders even then,
proud to go down in the strafing storms
of winter, always ahead of the prow.

Across waves I've traveled backward
to now—to what remains of Rome,
where weeks of November rains

have brought the smell of mold
instead of frost. Thick curtains
leave their ancient must
on the hands that draw them closed;
I learn again that water can be hard:
it whitens pans and yellows whites
and heavies my head with unrinsed hair;
soaps foam flat and form a scum
on bilge that runs down chalk-clogged drains
to timeless cloaca, the *caput* of a listless Italy
where beach towns perch and linger
along the ever-charming lee. *Il mare,*
they'll say here, for both, but a sea

is not always an ocean. Yet
what did I know of water
but steam from kettles, frost on panes,
snowflakes on the frozen lake? the melt
that soaked the roads to mud,
the taste of salt, the stinging
cleanness of my skin—not spore-spotted drapes
or contorted alleyways, but hard shutters
and doorways of pine—hard
as the fresh-swabbed decks
from which Nantucket sailors
must have beheld the expanse of time
and the weight of Ahab's lone Atlantic,
crashing gray and white on pebbled shores.

The Old Man and the Hills

On the restaurant terrace of the Castle in the Clouds
a little girl plays scissors, paper, rock
with her young father, whose eyes when they meet mine
are guarded and defiant in the way
of New Hampshire men, men
who taught me the fight in faces like his
when I was younger than this girl.
These tiny towns spread out below, I know them still—

towns with yards whose well-mown lawns
abut the frost-heaved roads,
where box-spring coils and rust-hulled sedans
squat on blocks of cement,
where half-roofed barns house short frayed cords,
split wires and headless nails—
all manner of useless things no native would claim
 won't someday be put to use.

Twelve years ago when the ancient rock came loose
the stony mascot who marks the roads
finally lost his granite jaw: The Old Man of the Mountain
became a lie. Up here I see what was never there,
a fairy gondola I hung from the mists in these hills
—these hills I thought were mountains.
The parapets I placed at the top dissolve
as the whims of a failed magnate, his aerie
built and lost and gained again,
but now only for visitors—
city folk like me whom I still loathe,
stuck behind them on these winding roads.

The young father finishes his beer in quick drafts,
keeping one hand free
for his daughter. I've tried to turn away,

he knows I'm watching him
keeping the wizening seasons at bay.
Decades ago, my father would refuse to lose
the games he taught me to play,
War, and Sorry! and Steal the Old Man's Pack.
Improbably, this girl is winning
game after game, smooth hand blanketing
her father's granite bluffs,
little fist crushing the twin blades of his shears,
steel fingers cleaving his flat palm in two
as though they've done this all her summers and falls,
switching roles but never changing odds.

Last week I found my father on YouTube,
still strumming the strings of his dolorous life
but much closer to earth than I remember.
I'm forty-nine today. His old man chin grizzles,
his neck-flesh sags, while my eyes are blue
as this September sky—this glorious day
of a child whose joy
has softened her father's frozen gaze. Improbably,
I believe I've won.

Why do you squander / Why do you hoard?

1

Fashion a necklace, frame a mirror,
imagine an ocean in a conch,

palp the palate
for a faintly remembered taste:

there's no sound
for extinction.

The waves you hoped to hear
are the rush of the mind in the inner ear

—the absent gastropod
whose gelatinous muscle

once pulsed inside—
anus, tentacle, auricle, gill,

a self whose stomach
was also its foot.

2

An osprey eyes its messy nest;
a heron's neck beckons
with its white question:

who'd have guessed
I'd comb this beach one fall,
the shell-strewn desert-sea

some call Cortez? A circle below
the murderers, Dante met men
who chose to sin against themselves,

forbidden to possess
the bodies they thought were their own
—*not for us to dwell within again.*

3

What chimeras, then,
are these? Silurian,

Ordovician: this sliver
a worm, this protrusion
an anemone,

their salt-bleached skeletons
infinitesimally becoming sand

among plastic beer cups
and eviscerated cod.

Virgil didn't give them long,
or maybe they had nothing to say.

4

Tendon, corpuscle, ligature,
bonecage keeping me standing
scanning the Pacific's patient millennia,

what did I imagine
but a way of leaving
something pure behind?

Place them
wherever you please,
they sought annihilation, only to find

their souls stuck in eternal
rehearsal. Early on a man told me
Try it once, you'll try again,

we always do. Run your hands
along the corrugated surfaces. Life
has never been delicate.

Vigil

There is a window that appears

in his hot sleep, its shutters thrown wide

but the frame is painted shut. Beyond, hills where gentians

bloom in manure, where angelica and yarrow twist

among the rock-strewn herbs;

where sometimes a small unicorn bends its neck,

munching flowers or tart apples in the new grass

though he can't taste their cider. Tonight

the heavy blankets hem

his long twisting body, one long bare leg

thrust out to feel the winter air. Sometimes I fear

he's breathing wrong—fitful silences, propulsive exhalations

—searching for the word he needs

and can't get out. From him I learned the words

for the thistle whose stem can be cooked to tenderness

and the purple trifoliate clover

that bites like sweet onion. With him, I've seen

the Mont Blanc in the *clair de lune*, seen rills that cool

the dry-hot, blanched-gold fields. Most nights I hope

to dream in the tongue of his childhood:

> *Fenêtre*, he'll murmur; *Window*, I'll hear

and it will open at my touch.

Ashes, Ashes

Julia says *I'm so sick of sand in my house*
   breaking another vacuum cleaner. No more
shells, Ruthie knows, no copper whelk
   or bearded cowrie, no mulberry sponge
or creamy auger, though *(Hold these, Manna)*
   she's busy anyway, my pockets are wet,

she's gathering arrow-head sand dollars
   washed up with evening's low waves
and amassed among the gray-black rock
   at the far end of the darkening beach.
Not the delicate discs I see, hearing
   sand dollar, or used to see—they're huge,

palm-sized, the once-living limbs now
   elongated almonds, reshaping the sea
I knew. Here's a perfect half-specimen!
   I'll have to hold it in my hands or crush it.
But Ernie's grimacing, wet lashes turned
   from our fun: he's dropped a shell-

encrusted stone on his foot. Wants to go
   toast the sunset back home, a shot glass
all his own, juice refilling with every ching-
   ching. Soon, edges will thin out, soften
(Mama and I will have gin), but wait—
   Ruthie's found another, almost

symmetrical, outlines of all five legs
   unbroken, little amygdalae. Ruthie,
I've no room left, and we can't take them
   with us, remember? but Mama is here,
by the ebbing waves, Ernie's laughing
   and we dance a family ring

around the inscrutable rosey— You know
   it's about the Plague—Yes, I know—
so what? we're spinning, the earth is too
and now   with glee   We all   fall
   down! —small wet butts in cool wet sand,
in my heavy pockets skeletons like stars.

Where We Are

The Whitney, Fall 2018

"And it was all I had, so I drew it,"

said Elsie Driggs. Clifford Still,

pictured here with all his paint,

said "I never wanted color to be color."

And God asked Minnie Evans

"Why don't you draw, or die?"

(She drew.)

I want words to be words

the way my cat wants a shifting patch of light to be a bird

she'll never catch. All that scrabbling, bare floor.

All Elsie had was a Pittsburgh mill:

"This shouldn't be beautiful," she said. But

Minnie's *Airlie Oak*'s in leaf, here

on this white wall,

Clifford's color blooms,

fuchsia fire after blue; ivory fire, green, always fire

still burning, like Elsie's black factory:

shouldn't be.

Is.

Note

"Invasive" incorporates language from Brenda Hillman's "Little Furnace," the opening poem of *Bright Existence.* The lines referred to are "a thousand insects outside called // and made me nothing"; and "the world was created to comprehend itself // as matter." Hillman also describes Mary as "white as a sand dollar."

Hillman's poems exist in dialogue with the Gnostic Gospels, combining metaphysical and lyric modes as they explore the relationship between inner wisdom and the physical world. The complex cosmology of the Gnostics has come to haunt me, particularly in light of our unabated destruction of the earth.

Acknowledgements

I am grateful to the editors of the literary journals where the following poems first appeared:

Spoon River Poetry Review: "And the stars" (as "Covenant") and "Where We Are"
Lily Poetry Review: "Past Perfect"
LEON Literary Review: "Love at 24" and "Love at 48"

*

Thank you to my teachers, who helped me consider my work worth their time and careful attention: Stephen Dobyns, Sandra Lim, Christine Kitano, Gaby Calvocoressi, and Alan Shapiro—and Deb Allbery and Ellen Bryant Voigt at Warren Wilson. More recently, to Sandra Beasley, whose instincts and savvy, generosity and graciousness helped shape a shaggy bunch of poems into a collection.

To Eileen Cleary, poet, teacher, editor, and poetic citizen extraordinaire, whose trust in me and my work has been vital, far beyond bringing this book into the world. And to my dearest friends, for helping bend my arc back towards life: Dionis, Gale, Amy, and Maxx.

Thank you to Colin and Julia, who have shared their little ones—Ruthie, Ernie, Callum, and hurricanes Ian and Tillie—with their adoring aunt. Thank you to those little ones for recounting the elaborate plots of movies, guiding me through the punchlines of extremely complicated jokes, and tolerating the kinds of questions their parents know not to ask.

To Majo and my mother and Timmy, who are altogether too proud. And to Greg—hero of these poems, hero of my life.

About the author

Since receiving her MFA from the Warren Wilson Program for Writers in January 2020, Amanda Shaw has been a caretaker for her mother. A teacher for over 20 years, she also works as an editor at the World Bank and is the book review editor for *Lily Poetry Review*. Though she has lived in Brooklyn, Detroit, Geneva, and Rome, she currently divides her time between New Hampshire, where she was born, and Washington, D.C.